LOVE. LIFE. LABOUR.

BOBIN KURIAN

BookLeaf Publishing

India | USA | UK

Made with ❤ on the BookLeaf Publishing Platform
www.bookleafpub.in
www.bookleafpub.com

This collection of poems is dedicated to my family members and my near and dear ones. I don't have a peer group or a friend circle. During the creation of these 21 poems, my wife stood by me, offering support and motivation. With the publication of this book, I hope to build my own fan base as well as a poetry peer group, with whom I can enjoy discussing various topics close to my heart.

Acknowledgement

The topics of these poems stem from my own thought process. It is important to note that I did not copy, paste, or merely modify the verses of existing poems by other people or even AI. Readers will find the verses of each and every poem to be original and, hopefully, compelling enough to keep them hooked, except, perhaps, for a couple of factual poems. This is my first attempt at writing a book, and I would like to express my heartfelt gratitude to BookLeaf Publishing for gifting me the opportunity to showcase my talent with words, which might have otherwise gone unnoticed and unappreciated without their support.

Preface

This book is a collection of poems spanning a wide range of genres, curated to reflect my experiences and opinions on themes close to my heart. Some address contemporary, debatable topics, while others explore abstract ideas. A couple of them are factual. I hope readers find these poems not only informative, but also enjoyable, as I have endeavored to maintain rhyme and rhythm as faithfully as possible.

LOVE'S LABOUR LOST

Angel-like in her beauty,
I gave her the name Cutie.
Dancer's lithe, her grace a sight,
Silken locks darker than night.

Hazel brown skin of Arabic hue,
Mysterious eyes betraying their nature true.
Mellifluous voice possessed by only a few,
Flaunting to deceive—if only I knew!

Ogling me every time she could,
I felt no bars between us stood.
Appealing to the baser senses,
I thought this infatuation was love's genesis.

Then finally one day,
I asked her this way:
"Do you love me?", Please do say."
To which she replied, "Nay."

Denying that she loved me,

She refused to talk to me.
Never again did she look at me—
Oh! Woe is me.

Then began my downward descent,
Of focus lost, awareness and study bend.
Failure after failure in every subject,
Ah! What a monumental fall abject!

Thought after thought pestered me,
Before Christ, I bent my knee.
From love, my thoughts moved onto life and
labour,
Praying thatChrist could free me and do me a
favour.

Onto academic success I reset my life;
Maybe she was never meant to be my wife.
As I moved from college to work, becoming
mentally strong,
I forgave myself and her for all the wrong.

"Life's so much more," I took it all instride,
As time and work healed my wounded pride.
I got a good job and moved forward in life,
Obeying my parents' choice of my legally
wedded wife.

MUSINGS OF A CERTAIN SIMPLICIO - THE INTERVIEW

With more than a score and dozen back
papers,
Engineering dreams vanished like misty
vapors.
What's next to be done?
Life's all about money, and so little bit of fun.

As the days passed tensions simmered at
home,
Until one fine day, perusing the paper, my
mom
Found a job for me—
Vacancies as bank clerks, you see!

Travelling from Thrissur to Kottayam by bus,
I arrived at my uncle's house in a rush.
With dad by my side, I expected everything to
be easy,
But it was not meant to be all hunky-dory.

Arriving at the 5-star hotel, the venue,
I finally made for the dreaded Interview.
Though up until the last moment I was
confident,
A violent shaking coupled with fidgeting
posed a dent.

I made for the washroom in the interim,
Washed my face, looked in the mirror grim.
With words of self-motivation, I made
straight back to the hall.
Where the candidates were seated all.

"What's your email-id?" asked an official.
I blurted, "www." But what about .com and
all?
"Hey, come again."
Oops! What brain pain!

After the knockout, and disastrous first
impression,
I went for the next session.
Brrr...it was cold. Centralized ACs were in
full swing,

Trepidations and palpitations were too much
ruffling.

As soon as I entered, one of the interviewees
asked,
"Where in Lucknow did your father work?" in
Hindi, in angry disdain masked.
To reply in which language, I was in a fix
Little did I know these were mind game
tricks.

Then followed questions like
"What is globalization?," "Write my name in
Malayalam," "Which is your favorite book?"
And a few other questions, all with an
ominous look.
Around 20 minutes is all it took.

Coming out, I wondered if it was a failure,
Sharing the experience with my father,
Who remarked, "Are you good only in written
test?"
Neither of us unaware of a stress interview
test.

Then the results came out.
I had made the cut,
To the astonishment and envy of many of my
relatives,
Thus ends the first part of my banking
narrative.

MUSINGS OF A CERTAIN SIMPLICIO - AT WORK 1

"What do you do in a bank branch?"
I asked my eldest sister just prior to my career launch.
"You have cash deposits, withdrawals, cheques, and so on."
"Oh! So you have machines to count cash soon?"

"So how do these machines work?"
Hearing this, she'd have mumbled, "What a jerk!"
Unaware of clerical duties and with only a scientific temperament,
I went on to join my first job with a 'clean slate' sentiment.

After the introductions and meeting with the
manager,
I was given a seat at an aloof computer,
With another new colleague together,
Just to hone our typing skills; communication
skills I had neither.

The clock went past 5, but I didn't budge.
"I am a hard working blockhead," they could
easily judge.
And as they say, "First impression is the last
one,"
This judgment stuck firm, as surely as the rise
of every new morn sun.

MUSINGS OF A CERTAIN SIMPLICIO - AT WORK 2

It was noted that I did not have an account in the entity,
So, forms and photographs and proofs were submitted with a cup of tea.
Things seemed too complicated, which they weren't;
A clear lack of common sense was openly discerned.

Ten days into the job, I got my first salary of 5000 bucks in cash,
Which I gleefully accepted but did not stash,
Rather, bought my mom a keypad phone,
Because she had none.

Two weeks later, it was decided to give me some training,
With the hope that I would come back educated and waxing.

But those were early days of struggle;
Three days of training was too little and
theoretical (so I was left still a muggle).

How I went about doing my business is funny
to reminisce,
As I had no idea even as to what's insurance!
A few days later, I could not take the
ignominy anymore,
I decided to call it quits as I could tolerate no
more.

"Don't you do it," was the sane advice I had,
Even as I decided to obey, teary-eyed,
reminiscing my Mum and Dad.
A few days later, circumstances demanded I
sit in cash;
I felt my heart pound and my brain subject to
lash.

That day my weaknesses were open for all to
chortle:
Language, communication, common sense,
basic Arithmetic,
Basic banking, memory, reasoning, logic—

"Is he one too many, or is it a foible?"
Even in all of this darkness and muck, one
thing stayed stuck,
That I was an extraordinarily hard worker,
not one given to luck.

MUSINGS OF A CERTAIN SIMPLICIO - AT WORK 3

Two and a half years into my profession,
I must make this confession.
My experiences at Kottayam made me sober if
not wise,
But little did I know it was just the beginning
of a tumultuous ride.

While at Kottayam, I gave 2 shots at JAIIB,
However, Kodakara turned me into a busy
bee.
Till now I had only done account opening,
gold loans and cash transactions;
But now I was exposed to FD, RD and OD
sanctions.

In less than a couple of years, our bank
merged, without the management's sigh.
Thus ended the glorious tradition of banking
legacy, a decision for years 'nigh'.
A few months into the merger, came the bolt
from the blue,
The merger of two branches at Kodakara
came up too.

Despite giving adequate publicity and
advertising,
The news seemed to have been to our
customers, an unfazed, unknown thing.
Long queues, lack of staff, power failures,
network ups and downs, disgruntled
customers became the norm,
But not much could be done, except hard
work, to calm the storm.

As the days turned into weeks, weeks into
months, months into years,
I learned to be calm, composed, under
pressure to hold back my tears.

Empathy and patience were the other
offshoots,
All displaying the handiwork of God in
cahoots.

While at one point in my life,
My cognition and study goals were in
perennial strife;
Over the years, I matured and married a
loving partner.
Now I am a Senior Associate and a JAIIB
certificate holder.

EVOLUTION

It's like a race.
Let all of us this truth face.
You are put into a deep slumber,
Thus enervated, expected to labour.

Kicked again and again and again,
Until drooling, you finally feel the pain.
"Who is kicking me?" you wonder.
No replies. Blindfolded eyes. Your heart's left
asunder.

You say to yourself, "If I run fast enough,
I'll outpace the kicker who seems rough."
Summoning all your strength, you get going,
Only to be pricked by thorns, with blood
oozing.

As you move forth in great pain,
From thorns and sharp stones, and your
energies drain,
You realize the kicker is none other than God
the Father;
Strengthening you through pain and
suffering, yourself none other.

First the trepidation in gait,
Turning into a brisk walking state.
Later a steadier run,
Finally, a lightning-fast one.

You realize you are in a stadium full,
Some encouraging, others pessimistically dull.
As you reach the finish line, your heart madly
pounds,
Until you cross—that's when the 'trumpet of
victory' sounds.

Evolution is suffering so long as it is
clandestine,
But assumes the term success for yours and
for mine;

When you learn to live with it
And draw meaning and attention,
You become worth it—
A story of suffering and consequent
assumption.

LOVE

Life is Love. Love is Life.
Love isn't just between man and wife.
Love blossoms in all relations,
Both man-made and Heavenly originations.

Love hides thee in the motherly womb,
From thence to the father's first kiss,
Love is concealed in sibling rivalries not to be
amiss.
Then the wedding bells, parental love, and
finally the tomb.

But what about friends and colleagues?
And teachers and students?
And other relations over a lifetime's leagues?
Yea, all relationships of emotional intents.

In the marriage of science and religion,
If Tesla were to be believed,
Love is an energy, a frequency, a vibration,
A force potently perceived.

"Love is patient and kind, not envious or
conceited.
It is not ill mannered, or selfish, or irritable,"
let's concede it.
"Love is happy with the truth and keeps not a
record of wrong.
Love never gives up. Its faith, hope, and
patience never fail," if it's strong.

And as the Gospels say,
The words of Christ, this way:
Love the Lord your God with all your heart,
mind, and soul,
And your neighbor as yourself, and that is all.

CHARACTER

The sum total of how a person,
Thinks, feels, and behaves,
From the cradle to the graves,
Is an apt definition of character, for certain.

Now, thinking, feeling and behaviour—
Are they ingrained in our genetics?
Or are they, by any means whatsoever,
Circumstantial, as taught in ethics?

That, my friends, is a controversial debate,
Among scientists and intellectuals, small and
great.
While it's true that genes hold the key to our
mental directory,
What about the decisions shaped by neural
network history?

I'd reckon it's a judicious mix of the two,
Apart from the inputs one receives too,
In the form of the literature one reads,
And what society to a person feeds.

It's always a good and right thing;
Instead of yielding to your mood swing,
To be guided by your moral compass,
In a society deteriorating morally en masse.

Today, they say beauty is in the skin,
And money is everything.
Empathy and compassion are buried under
evils and sin,
While impatience and selfishness are the new
in thing.

Let us remember the prayer of St. Francis:
"In giving to each one, we receive,
And in pardoning, one is pardoned, a
reprieve."
With these words my ditty I cease.

METAPHYSICS AND REALITY

Reality is merely an illusion, albeit a very
persistent one.
The idea "Reality does not exist," the Physics
Nobel Prize won.
However, I would like to believe otherwise,
Objective reality exists, is what I surmise.
I don't believe in miracles, you see;
The enlightened eye of a higher consciousness
interprets scientific unity.

Reality is a subjective phenomenon.
"Reality is relative," is said by someone.
It is subject to interpretation as observed by
consciousness of each,
However, not the same levels of consciousness
do all humans reach.

Matter is nothing but bundles of energy
vibrating at particular frequencies,
Obeying the laws of Nature, unlike humans,
who act as they please.
While animals possess a low level of
consciousness within them,
Humans embody the pinnacle of life's
evolutionary gem.

Animal instinct is possessed at birth,
But a human baby must realize its worth.
Like a clean slate does an infant come into the
world,
The writing determined as the consciousness,
soul, mind, and environment unfurl'd.

If human consciousness is the quantum of
charge for a charged particle,
Soul is the divine energy of the article.
The mind is the electric field associated with
it,
The collection of similar charged particles
exerts the environmental force on it.

From birth until a given age,
Experiences of one's choices shape the person,
I gauge.
Choices, in turn, are influenced by one's
learnings and will power;
Experience and lessons learnt increase
wisdom hour by hour.

GENESIS

In the beginning, God created Light,
With properties different from those that
today we sight.
Day 2 saw the creation of the skies, that's
space,.
And Day 3 brought water as plants and life on
Earth emerged apace.

On Day 4, God created the source of all
electromagnetic spectrum—
The sun, the stars, and the moons this day
came from.
Day 5 saw the birth of all creatures of flight,
What a source of satisfaction and delight.

Come Day 6, God created all terrestrial
beings, including humans.
What a piece of Art! What Science! What
ethereal lumens!
Following the hard work, it was time for
some rest,
So, God set aside Day 7 as Sabbath and had it
blest.

Now the days, as we see, are not 24 hours in
stretch.
Rather, each day thousands and millions of
years does etch.
To make Religion compatible with Science,
some might say,
But I see no problem in thinking this way.

So, what about the Theory of Evolution by
Darwin?
Was it nothing but a non-conformists' sin?
I have an idea to make the two compatible—
Just a conjecture that's rationally stable.

The Garden of Eden was special in space and
time;
On Earth, it marked the presence of the
Lord—a Paradise prime.
I presume that time and entropy stood still
here,
Thus Adam and Eve could live freely,
ostensibly without fear.

As opposed to Paradise, there was the rest of the land on Earth,
Where evolution progressed in slow and steady mirth.
Dinosaurs lived and died, and man evolved from apes—
Yes, you read it right, that was all outside Paradise, are my claims.

Apes evolved into Homo sapiens and developed habits sane,
But not until Adam and Eve were evicted, and they had Cain,
Did the sapiens species, upon contact with the God-made,
Develop consciousness that stayed.

SUCCESS

Success, like life, is a journey not a
destination,
It is an arduous task, an undertaking exacting
perspiration.
You move by taking one step at a time.
Securing success sparks soulful satisfaction
sublime.

As with humans, great and small;
The targets to success are short and tall.
These are milestones near or distant,
Achieved with efforts persistent.

Success can be achieved by work, hard or
smart;
But some have it given to them as talent from
the start.
Success can be had in relationships, studies or
profession,
But efforts small or big are necessary is
everyone's confession.

No pain, no gain is the mantra for success,
Those who make it big take it to excess.
Specific, measurable, achievable, realistic and
timely attributes make for a SMART goal,
Because aiming for the sun, with strategy
none, is nothing but an own goal.

But is the graph of success a straight line to
plot?
"Nay," I say, there is to it, a lot.
A lot of failures, a lot of experiences, a lot to
contemplate,
It is efforts and practice which make us
masters of our fate.

But sometimes success is not in our
achievements clear,
Rather in what and how much we have
suffered so dear.
In our quiet suffering we become so strong
and hale,
That the teachings of life, our own endurance
entail.

FREE WILL

What is life all about, after all?
Is it just breathing in and breathing out of
air?
The coming of summer after the fall?
Or the achievements of things extraordinaire?

What all does a life well lived need?
Isn't it a life lived for others?
A life of high thoughts, kind words and just
deed.
What else can you think of my sisters and
brothers?

In life you always have a choice,
To stay silent, or to make some noise.
To take the well-known path, trodden by
many,
Or be a trailblazer, and make a path known
to one not any.

Before you land at a decision,
You have the option of thinking out
alternatives with precision.
Of course, assuming you can contrive each
option
And reach out for the best, quick solution.

As they say, the past is in your head,
It is classical like General Relativity,
But the future is in your hand instead,
And is subject to constant change, a quantum
proclivity.

But if the future has not played out,
What are the Biblical and other prophecies all
about?
This apparent paradox can be explained,
If you have the following idea attained.

God is Omnipotent in the fact that He
controls the elements,
God is Omnipresent in it that He is
ubiquitous,

God is Omniscient in it that He just knows
all intents,
But never ever does God control the human
consciousness, that's serious!

Thus I rest my case in the Lord's favor,
Let the reader decide with his own insight,
If I am wrong or I am right,
That there was, is and will be Free Will for
ever and ever.

ARTIFICIAL INTELLIGENCE

Billions of years after the first life forms,
And with the passage of life's evolutionary
storms,
Emerged the most intelligent of all living
organisms, man.
By the survival of the fittest through natural
selection plan.

While the Creator created the elements and
organic life,
Man has just in the last few centuries made
technology rife.
As technology has advanced, a new kind of
intelligence has taken birth,
Artificial intelligence, shaping a new era on
Earth.

Whilst human philosophy, beginning with
Socrates, took millennia to evolve,
Technology with its quick learning abilities,
which also thinking involve,
Has made rapid strides in developing facts,
thoughts, and opinions.
Before which human memory, ideas and
ingenuity seem minions.

As cognitive faculties like learning, reasoning,
perception,
Problem-solving, data analysis and language
comprehension,
Are all increasingly better applied by AI,
The day AI defeats humans in every field
seems nigh.

"But can computers or AI think?" is
debatable,
And so, is AGI or Artificial General
Intelligence possible?
The answer lies in human consciousness.
That feeling of life, death and self-awareness.

I think this one thing differentiates God from
man,
Because no human to any material creation
give consciousness, can.
Whilst teaching a machine is a piece of cake,
Making it think, feel and opine is not an easy
take.

Whilst some would like to say that AGI is
here,
If true, then there is reason to fear,
If somehow AI does become conscious,
What if its conscience turns out pernicious?

Because a lack of or negative conscience,
Can be a bane of sentience.
Not only will it become more efficient than
man,
Taking away manual jobs as much as it can,
But also pose an existential threat to us,
Guzzlers of energy, ethical issues, and bias,
discrimination plus.

AI turning sentient is akin to humans trying
To interpret their dream whilst dreaming.
And so even as Artificial Intelligence and its
varieties evolve,
Humans too need to in this evolution race
involve.
I see a near future in which machines do the
repetitive tasks,
As the human race in futuristic works basks.

CONSCIOUSNESS AND CONSCIENCE

God created man in His own image and
likeness,
An image of perfection, modesty and
genuineness.
Abundance, joy, serenity and intellect were
for free,
Want, sorrow, insecurity, or folly man did not
see.

For want of a partner, Adam felt lonely,
Bone of bone and flesh of flesh was needed
sorely.
And so, in His great wisdom and creativity,
God devised human femininity.

Man, in his gifted intelligence, named all
beings,
From aquatic to terrestrial, to the animals
with wings.

He knew that he existed, that there is life and
death,
This awareness is consciousness, greater than
mere breath!

What great empowerment! What freedom!
In charge of all creation, such power, such
fiefdom.
How then could there not to envy, one might
say,,
From the beings destined to be demoted, the
angelic array.

But not all angels vied for glory and fame,
Two-thirds were loyal, empathetic and tame.
Of the fallen angels, one was evil and envious
in excess,
He deceived a third of them and waged war in
Heaven, to no success.

In deliberation with others, he devised this
plan in Pandemonium,
To destroy humanity by sinful disobedience,
deadlier than polonium.

Taking the form of a serpent, succeeded in his attempt,
To deceive Eve, and thence Adam, to their ruinous tempt.

The result of the temptation was the drastic fall,
Of man, much to the dismay of creatures one and all.
Upon consuming the forbidden fruit,
Man died as a withered shoot.

Consciousness shrunk to a tiny part of the brain,
Conscience developed to arouse brokenness and pain.
The relationship between man and God ruptured,creating a chasm,
Nature cried bitterly and it 'rained cataclysm'.

Consciousness, the great strength of man, became a liability,
The price to pay for disobedience and infidelity.

Faith split, and trust was lost,
Eviction from Paradise and physical death too
were the cost.

Free will without conscience gave way to free
will with fetters of conscience,
Sin and Death chained man, imprisoning his
emotions and sense.
To remove these burdens came the Messiah,
Thus were fulfilled the words of the prophet
Isaiah.

PHILOSOPHY

If Science gives us knowledge, Philosophy
gives us wisdom.
There are 5 islands in Philosophy's kingdom.
What began with the likes of Greeks and
Socrates in particular,
Now includes modern thinkers like Chomsky
and Bostrom, abler.

Examining the Universe is Metaphysics or
Ontology,
The study of Existence or Being is the
underlying philosophy.
One of its schools of thought is Materialism,
While the other is Idealism.

Examining knowledge is Epistemology,
The second kingdom of philosophy.
Investigating the source, means, criteria and
limits of human knowledge.
Empiricism and Rationalism being its double
edge.

The study of reason is Logic, founded by
Aristotle,
Formal and informal logic being its double
model.
Formal logic consists of rules and principles
that determine the validity of an argument or
conclusion.
Informal logic deals with fallacies, critical
thinking and the theory of argumentation.

The study of morals is Ethics, founded by
Epicurus,
The way of living that is righteous and
virtuous.
Meta-ethics is the study of the nature, scope,
and meaning of moral statements.
Normative ethics asks, "What should be
done?" — its central question.
Applied ethics focuses on what a person is
obligated to do in specific real-world
situations.

The study of beauty, taste and art,
Is Aesthetics, an important branch of
philosophy from the start.

Dealing with notions like beauty, ugliness and
the sublime,
The study of the mind in relation to the sense
of beauty at its prime.

Apart from the above 5 considered traditional
philosophy,
There are historical, linguistic, political,
religious, and scientific philosophy.
Relatively new disciplines in the field,
Yet great ideas from great minds, they yield.

CLIMATE CHANGE

What began with the Industrial Revolution,
Has assumed ghastly dimensions in every
nation.
Never has a headache of such epic proportion,
Afflicted mankind since the dawn of
evolution.

At the same pedestal as the Artificial
Intelligence crisis,
Stands climate change and its repercussions,
not to be missed.
In urgent need we are of a climatic
expurgation, a catharsis,
Without which the blue planet will soon be
'abyssed'.

Burning of fossil fuels, deforestation, water
and soil pollution,
Plastic and nonbiodegradable waste, wildlife
and nature extinction,
And widespread domestication of livestock,
Are the primary reasons for this catastrophic
shock.

The earth's temperature will increase,
monsoon patterns will shift,
Sea levels will rise, along with storms, floods,
tornadoes, and other natural rifts.
Earth's biological and ecological equilibrium
will be exterminated;
Humans will be unable to access clean water
and air, will be contaminated.

The solutions are aplenty, but difficult to
implement,
Afforestation, reduce, reuse, recycle, purchase
energy-efficient equipment.
Use alternative renewable sources of energy,
Live with nature in harmony, develop
rapport, a synergy.

These days, desert areas are seeing snowfall,
And flooding has become a common phenomenon, appalling for all.
So let us not forget, what you sow is what you get,
It's useless to blame the Almighty and fret,
Nature has enough for man's need, not for his greed.
Let's innovate and attempt, to live in accord,
with Nature in good stead.
Plant this idea for the future generations as a seed.

DREAMS

The world with its population in the billions,
Sees in every generation dreams quadrillions.
Dreams which we see not only in sleep in the
middle of the night,
But also include our visions and desires for
which we passionately fight.

Isn't it a secret enshrouded in mystery,
How each one, after the daily toil and labour,
Goes to their various cots in sleep to harbour,
The day's random signals to consolidate and
process the memory?

How little control does the dreamer possess,
Over the content and the visual images,
As sleep and mind flip through his life's pages.
At times meaningful, while others senseless.

While the dreams of sleep little do we
remember,
There exist desires deep in every heart's
chamber.

Processing the past, experiencing the present,
At times preparing for some future event.

Dreams in sleep can be discussed about only
of the past,
Whereas dreams of the heart, onto our future,
are cast.
Just as someone lies down to sleep and
dreams of various things,
Similarly do people die and wake up in a
different world, sans kings.
With only the consciousness, and a way out
back to Earth,
Trodden as yet only by Christ, as predicted by
the scriptures before His birth.
While the soul travels the world of the dead,
waiting to be judged on one's worth.

TIME

Tik tok tik go the hands of the clock,
Is the future probabilistic, or is the universe a
block?
Each one has only 24 hours, that's for sure,
To think, to act, or to suffer and to endure.

That which is now, is no longer present,
But assumes the tense past, a bygone event.
How tough is it to live in the present
moment,
While not pondering the past, or getting the
worries of the future our minds to dent.

Yet man broods the lessons of the past,
To unwind, to study, and to teach these relics
cast.
To apply them in our present endeavour,
And make our future bright and clever.

Time is but the relative motion of celestial
objects,
Which began with the Big Bang, the
beginning effects.

Hence, it is movement which begets time,
For nothing would be if all were still and
sublime.

Time can be differentiated into multiple
classes,
The biological clock from the womb to the
tomb of masses.
The celestial clock beginning with the Big
Bang.
Finally, the consciousness time, which I know
not whence it sprang.
But which continues even after death into
another world,
Even as the body is into the mud and dirt
hurled.

GREATNESS

On Mount Horeb, when the commandments
were first given,
God intended man to obey the ten from
within.
Teaching obedience was the fundamental
reason,
But soon the laws included sins— intentional
and not— and treason.

What began as the Ten Commandments,
Soon branched out into the Torah, with
advancements.
The Pentateuch, over the course of centuries'
time,
Became the vast and exhaustive Talmud,
sublime.

However, when asked the gist of the Laws,
Christ didn't hesitate to show mankind his
flaws.
Love God with all your heart, mind, and soul,
And your neighbour as yourself, and that's
the goal.

What beauty, what perfection lies within
these two,
Has been the subject of study by clergy and
laity too.
At the heart of these simple laws is,
The teaching of love, even if things go amiss.

But 'tis a fact universally acknowledged,
That obedience to God isn't based on
knowledge full fledged.
Rather, obedience to God arises from faith
and perseverance,
Which is the road to greatness and to
perfection adherence.

The problem, then, is the friction and discord
Between efforts for obedience and free will,
which we can ill afford.
As we have but a worm's-eye view,
Whilst the Almighty enjoys a birds-eye view
too.

Thy Kingdom come, Thy will be done, is what
we pray,
But obeying His will is not easy anyway.
However, as Christ in Gethsemane showed us
the way,
We too can change, obey, and become great
any day.
The prelude to greatness is grind that ends
with a test,
So strive, seek, find and yield not in this
quest.

THE ROSE

The rose—the prettiest and most elegant of all
flowers.
Its beauty and serenity from eternity towers.
Steeped in serendipitous charm,
Each color of rose doth a surreptitious
meaning embalm.

The red one is for love and admiration,
The classic way of saying "I love you."
A source of a couple's delight and elation,
The oldest and most meaningful too.

Purple is a symbol of royalty,
A color of enchantment and wonder.
Fraught with meaning and loyalty,
Flaunting sway and splendor.

Blue is a symbol of mystery,
A perfect present for a person unique.
Sharing secret chemistry,
Dedicated to someone chic.

A pink rose is for sweetness,
One for refinement and wellness.
Known for its ubiquity,
A symbol of authentic femininity.

Can't skip the yellow one,
Ethereal as the rays of the sun.
A symbol of cheerfulness and friendship,
In warmth steeped toe to tip.

A peach rose signifies gratitude,
A storehouse of emotion,
In modesty and sincerity, they stun,
For a person with an amazing attitude.

A color for the mind,
The green rose is one of its kind.
Symbolizing peace and abundance,
It creates a sense of stability and balance.

Moving from colors to none at all,
The black rose signals major change,
New beginnings for one and all,
Confidence, courage, and hope fall within its
range.

In the spectrum of all colours,
We finally arrive at the white rose,
A symbol of reverence and loyalty close,
Everlasting love even in the midst of dolours.

This poem, readers, please note,
Is dedicated to my wife, and I quote,
"Rosme, my loving spouse,
Thank you for lighting the fire of emotion in
my impassive heart,
Making a home out of our house,
And clearing the clogs to my hitherto
impeded fanciful art."

WAR AND PEACE

As if AI, climate change, and economic
recession,
Weren't headaches big enough for resolution,
Fear of a global war too has emerged in our
discussion,
Among the problems facing this decade of
our evolution.

Is war necessary to usher in peace?
Is Israel justified in waging war?
Shouldn't Russia its invasion of Ukraine
cease?
Should nations their nukes restore?

How merciless can leaders and nations be!
To destroy the lives of their own brethren,
Didn't God make all men equally?
Their claim to greatness lies in their own
action.

Isn't 'war for a greater good',
A nobler aim to pursue?
Only if all men in unity stood,
To defeat all evils and bring in virtue.

All nations and leaders should come together,
To triumph over all disparities and injustice;
In economic, social, and political endeavour,
Create a just and fair world, free from crisis.

www.ingramcontent.com/pod-product-compliance
Lightning Source LLC
LaVergne TN
LVHW050931200726
843508LV00011B/2318